The Entrepreneur's Video Tool Guide

DISCOVER THE FASTEST, CHEAPEST, AND EASIEST WAY TO START CREATING PRO-QUALITY BUSINESS VIDEOS USING LOW-COST AND NO-COST TOOLS AND TECHNIQUES

DAVID POWER

POWER MEDIA GROUP

BROOKLYN, NEW YORK

David Power/ Power Media Group
Brooklyn, NY
davidpower.com

Book Layout ©2013 BookDesignTemplates.com

The Entrepreneur's Video Tool Guide
David Power – 1st ed.
ISBN: 978-1539964650

Contents

DOWNLOAD THE AUDIOBOOK FREE

THANK YOU!

As a sincere thank-you for reading this book, I invite you to download the unabridged audiobook version of *The Entrepreneur's Video Tool Guide*.

Follow the link below for FREE instant access:

http://davidpower.com/evtg-audiobook

Section One

Introduction

[1]

Who Is This Book For?

THIS BOOK MAKES three broad assumptions about you as a reader:

1. You're a small business owner or entrepreneur.

2. You're interested in creating videos to build relationships with prospective customers and to promote your products and services to them.

3. You have little to no prior experience in video production.

If you just read all three points and said, *"Yup"*, silently in your head after each one, then this book was written with you in mind.

When I began making videos almost a decade ago, a book like this didn't exist. Instead, I spent close to 1,000 hours reading blog posts, newsletters, online forums and manufacturer's websites to find the tools I needed to produce a high-quality video.

Thankfully, your path will be much faster and smoother. First of all, audio and video gear and software are much easier to find and much more affordable now compared to when I started. But more importantly, the fact that I've condensed close to a decade's worth of research and trial and error into this short book means you'll shave close to 1,000 hours off of your learning curve. That may sound like a bold claim, but it's absolutely true.

Without congratulating myself too much, this is the book I wish I had a decade ago.

WHAT WE'LL COVER

As the title suggests, this book focuses on video tools for entrepreneurs. While most video creators use a common core set of tools, we entrepreneurs often have very different priorities in terms of the types of videos we create, why we create them, how we use them, and where we use them. This book pays special attention to these differences.

Here's a sampling of what we'll cover:

- Discover the types of videos your business needs in order to be successful online, the differences between them, and which ones to focus on when starting out.

- Learn the hardware components you need in order to shoot high-quality videos.

- Discover the software applications required to capture, edit and process raw audio and video clips.

- Learn the factors to consider when choosing a video hosting platform.

- How to keep your video production budget to a minimum by leveraging components you already own.

THREE MYTHS DEBUNKED

In my experience as a video producer and coach, I've found that most entrepreneurs fully appreciate the benefits of using video to promote their businesses. But those same entrepreneurs are often reluctant to get started because they believe one or more of the following myths regarding video production:

1. **Making videos is too expensive.** It's all too easy to spend a lot of money on video production gear and software. But when you're starting out and your skills and experience are at their lowest levels, not even a million-dollar kit will help you. In this book, you'll discover how to start making videos with the lowest possible financial investment. You're always welcome to spend more money, but I make every effort to show you how and where to cut corners without limiting your ability to produce high-quality results.

2. **Making videos is too complicated.** No doubt, video production can be very complicated, but it doesn't have to be. This book reveals how to keep

your video kit, your shoots, and your post-production workflow as simple as humanly possible.

3. **It takes too long to learn what I need to know.** Becoming a Hollywood director can take well over a decade. But acquiring the skills to create video content that looks and sounds great, content you're proud of, and content that compels your prospective customers to exchange their money for your products and services... that doesn't need to take long at all. If you're a fast reader, you can literally be ready to make your first video a little over hour from now. It won't be Hollywood quality. But your journey will have begun.

This book dispels these three myths. By focusing on the exact tools you need (without a lot of industry jargon or filler material), this book helps you start making videos confidently in the fastest, cheapest, and easiest way possible.

CAUTION

So far in this book, I've given you a lot of rah-rah, feel-good, you-can-do-it-style encouragement. And I've meant every word of it. However, there's one caution I want acknowledge before we go any further and it's this:

Reading this book won't turn you an expert video producer.

I'm hoping you're not overly surprised by this statement. Yet it's only fair and right that we both begin this book with reasonable expectations.

There's no way a single book can turn you into an expert *anything*. This book—like an introductory book on any topic—is designed to give you a solid understanding of the basic terms, tools and techniques. Once you've finished reading, it's up to you to take the next step. If you were to ask me what that step should be, I'd tell you, *"Pull out your camera and hit record."* You'll never learn how to swim unless you get in the water.

Let's get in the water.

David Power
Brooklyn, New York – October 2016

[2]

Why Video Is Important

I F YOU'VE OWNED some form of computer, tablet, or smartphone for longer than a day, then you're well aware that video is one of the most popular forms of online content. While static text and images can convey information effectively, and audio-only content (podcasts, for instance) offer on-the-go convenience, no other type of digital content beats video for its ability to make a true connection with another human being.

For millions of years before the Internet existed, our species relied on in-person, physical encounters with other humans to determine who was a friend, and who was an enemy. Our ancestors did this by looking people in the eyes, listening to their voices, and observing their body language. You, me and virtually everyone we know rely on these same cues today to tell us who we can trust and who we should avoid.

And while it's not (yet) as effective as a physical encounter, video allows us to build virtual relationships with an audience by offering a two-dimensional display of the physical cues our species is genetically programmed to rely upon. These include:

- Eye contact

- Facial expressions

- Vocal intonation

- Body language

It's practically impossible for any other type of content to match the impact and influence a well-produced video can have on a viewer. And perhaps best of all, online video permits us to reach a far larger audience than we could ever hope to reach in person. And it works for us literally 24 hours a day, every day of the year.

HOW ENTREPRENEURS USE VIDEO

Here's a list of some of the more common ways you can use video to promote your products and services.

1. **Introduction / About** - The two most popular pages on any website are the default homepage and the *About* page. If you're lucky enough to have someone visit your website, don't miss the opportunity to get your face and voice in front of them with an introductory video. Use this to let them know who you are and how your products and services will help them.

2. **Video Sales Letters** - If you've purchased any sort of information product online in the past couple of years, it's likely you've encountered at least a few video sales letters. VSLs typically consist of text—sometimes combined with images and animation—and audio narration (known as a *voice over*). The fact that we see VSLs so frequently speaks to their effectiveness in converting casual browsers into customers. With a few inexpensive tools, you can begin creating your own VSLs quickly and easily.

3. **Landing / Sales Pages** - A landing or sales page is any web page designed to encourage a visitor to perform a single requested action. This *single action* often involves subscribing to an email list in exchange for a freebie of some sort—a PDF download, protected video, webinar registration, or something similar. In the case of a sales page, the single action is almost always, *click the Buy Now button*. Because all menus, sidebars, popups, and other distractions have typically been removed, landing and sales pages offer a great opportunity to put your smiling face and voice in front of a (somewhat) captive audience.

4. **Advertising** - Video advertising has grown quickly in the past few years. YouTube and Facebook are two of the bigger video ad venues, but more are coming to the table every year. Given its

popularity and growth, your business stands to benefit greatly from being able to create video advertisements quickly and cheaply.

5. **Tutorials** - There are few better ways to build authority and trust with an audience than to provide solutions to their problems. Whether the problem is how to create a pivot table in Microsoft Excel, train a dog to sit, or use a camera properly, a short video tutorial can do wonders for your online profile and email list building efforts.

6. **Webinars -** Whether live or pre-recorded, webinars have proven to be very effective sales tools. They typically combine a detailed free training session with a sales pitch for a course or another information product. Lucky for us, webinars rely on the same core tools and techniques as other types of video you'll create for your business.

7. **Online Courses** - Once you've successfully built an online following, one of the best ways to monetize your expertise is by creating and marketing an online course. As you're likely aware, online courses rely heavily on video largely because it has a higher perceived value than other forms of online content.

8. **Product Launches** - Once you have a high-ticket product to sell—whether it's a live event, online course, mastermind group or something similar—

one very effective way to build excitement and buzz is through a formal product launch sequence. This normally consists of a four-part video series that culminates in the product being officially available for sale. Crafting these launch videos, the stories they tell, and the anticipation they build is both an art and a science.

I hope this list has started you thinking about how and where you'll use video to promote your business. Provided your video content is well-produced, there's almost no limit to the reach and impact you can have.

[3]

Types Of Video

VIDEO CONTENT COMES in any number of different shape, sizes, styles, and flavors. As entrepreneurs, the videos we'll create will be some combination or variation of two main types. Here they are:

LIVE ACTION (ON-CAMERA)

Any time you stand (or sit) in front of a camera, look into the lens, and deliver a message to your audience, you're creating a live action video. Doing this properly requires a fair amount of preparation. It requires you to write a script, rehearse it, wear decent clothing, fix your hair, set up lights, run camera and audio gear, perform the material several times, and finally edit and package the video into something you're proud of.

This style of video allows your audience to virtually experience your human side. When done properly, live action video is powerful and can have a profound effect on your brand, your relationship with your prospective customers, and ultimately your business profitability.

SCREENCAST

Screencast is a generic term I'll use to describe any combination of the following content:

1. **Static slides with images and text.** These slides can be generated with PowerPoint, Keynote (both of which we'll discuss later in the book), or any other application that permits you to type text onto a full-screen background.

2. **Video recordings of your computer screen.** These recordings often capture a real-time, over-the-shoulder demonstration of a software tool or technique.

Even though the business owner doesn't appear on-screen, a screencast video almost always includes the entrepreneur's voice as narrator. Screencasts are typically used for instructional or educational purposes but they can also be used for Video Sales Letters.

A video sales letter or VSL is a special case of the screencast video. In its simplest form, a VSL consists of a series of slides containing static text and a voice over recording that narrates the text exactly as it's displayed without embellishment or further explanation.

Note: *Here's an example of a short VSL I use in one of my businesses:*

http://davidpower.com/vslsample

Live action and screencast videos both play important roles in the brand building and marketing of any business. As you may have guessed from the descriptions in this chapter, live action is by far the more elaborate, complex and (potentially) expensive of the two types.

Don't let that intimidate you. This book covers all the tools you'll need to successfully create both types of video.

Section Two

Hardware

[4]

Cameras

IT WON'T SURPRISE you that a camera is *the* essential tool to a video creator—much like a brush is to a painter or a chisel is to a sculptor. You can't capture video unless you own or have access to a video camera.

The type of camera you use isn't that important. Even the cheapest models on the market are capable of capturing in-focus, well-exposed, high-definition images. Money is no longer an obstacle to creating high-quality video.

Before we discuss my camera recommendations, let's review some of the more important and essential camera terms and features.

ESSENTIAL CAMERA FEATURES

If you're new to the world of video, the technical terms and jargon can be confusing. Let's remove the confusion with the following explanations. If you've used a camera (still or video) extensively in the past, these definitions will serve as a refresher.

SENSOR

In olden times, cameras captured images on some form of film. Film was (and still is) a plastic strip covered in layers of microscopic crystals that react when exposed to light. Once exposed, film is bathed in a series of chemicals that react with the crystals to create a negative image that can later be printed or projected.

Digital cameras are much less messy. Instead of film, they contain a sensor consisting of millions of tiny *pixels*—a term derived from *picture elements*. Each pixel converts light into an electrical signal representing the color and intensity of the light at that point. The camera's computer brain converts these signals into a series of ones and zeros, and then stores them to a memory card. No chemicals. No darkrooms. No negatives.

While there's a positive relationship between pixel count and image quality (i.e. *more* usually equals *better*), the overall size of a camera's sensor can be even more important than the number of pixels. The full-frame sensors found in high-end DSLRs and cinema cameras typically capture sharper, cleaner images than our camcorders and smartphones which often have tiny (but still high-definition) sensors.

RESOLUTION

This term refers to the number of pixels of visual information the camera records with every image it captures. Most consumer-level video cameras and smartphones have resolutions of 1920 x 1080 pixels. This is often known as 1080p (where the 'p' stands for *progressive*.) Cameras with 1080p resolution capture and store over two million pixels (i.e. 1920 multiplied by 1080) in every frame.

While some newer cameras, phones and tablets are capable of 4K resolution (3840 x 2160 pixels), this is not a requirement for the types of videos you'll create for your business. 1080p is not only perfectly adequate for our purposes, but it's also more cost-effective: lower resolution means smaller files and smaller files require less storage, less bandwidth and less computer processing power—all of which have an associated cost.

FOCUS

This is a concept you likely understand well. And if you're like me, out-of-focus images make you very unhappy. Without getting too technical, here's a small slice of science to explain how camera focus is achieved.

Light rays traveling through a camera lens converge at a single point inside the body of the camera. The location at which the rays converge depends on the length of the lens, the number of glass elements it contains, and its *aperture* (which we'll discuss below).

When light rays converge at a point either in front of or behind the camera's sensor, the image appears blurry. When they converge directly on the sensor's surface, the image is in focus.

Most modern cameras use sophisticated electronics and tiny motors to autofocus the lens accurately and reliably. Autofocus is often a great help but there are times when it gets in the way. We'll discuss that a little later as well.

EXPOSURE

Exposure is one of the more complex topics in the camera world. What makes it complicated is the fact that proper exposure relies not on a single factor, but the relationship between three distinctly different camera parameters. These three parameters form what's sometimes referred to as the *exposure triangle*. Before we discuss the triangle, let's define the camera parameters that comprise it:

Aperture

Inside your video camera's lens is a ring (usually formed by a series of overlapping blades) that expands and contracts to control the amount of light reaching the camera's sensor. When the aperture is set to a low value, the ring is wider and more light reaches the sensor. At higher values, the ring is smaller and less light gets through.

A camera operator might adjust the aperture for several different reasons including:

1. **To emphasize a single object.** You've undoubtedly seen photographs or video in which the background is completely blurred out while the subject in the foreground (human face or other) is

in perfect focus. This can be accomplished with a wide aperture.

2. **To keep more of the scene in focus.** If you want objects in both the foreground and background to be in focus, a smaller aperture can accomplish this.

Note: How much of the image is in focus at a given aperture value is referred to as Depth of Field.

3. **To achieve balanced exposure.** It's sometimes the case that the other parameters in the exposure triangle will be locked or constrained in some way, and proper exposure can be achieved only by adjusting the aperture. This will make more sense in a moment.

Note: While consumer-level video cameras give you at least some control over aperture, most smartphones and tablets have fixed apertures that cannot be adjusted. This makes the exposure triangle somewhat simpler but gives you less creative flexibility.

Shutter Speed

You can think of the camera's shutter as a blade or a flap that sits in front of the camera's sensor and prevents light from reaching it.

> **Note:** *Digital cameras don't contain blades or flaps, but these mechanical descriptions help simplify the explanation.*

When you click the shutter release on a still camera or the *record* button on a video camera, the shutter opens for a brief period of time to allow light to reach the sensor. Then it closes again.

The length of time the shutter remains open is the shutter speed. The longer the shutter is open, the more light reaches the sensor. When it closes more quickly, the sensor receives less light.

Here are some factors that impact the choice of shutter speed:

1. **To freeze fast-moving objects.** When photographing or filming an event with a lot of quick motion—a baseball game or car race, for instance—a fast shutter speed can freeze the action and capture moving objects (like a ball or a car) crisply without blurring.

2. **To smooth out moving objects.** A technique used by many landscape photographers—particularly those capturing waterfalls, lakes, or other bodies of water—is to mount the camera to a sturdy tripod and use a very slow shutter speed (often several seconds) to smooth out movement of the water. With this technique, waterfalls look like white silk and lakes look like mirrors.

3. **To avoid camera shake.** When using a camera without a tripod under low-light conditions, you'll want to keep the shutter speed fast enough so that neither the movements of your subject nor your own small body movements result in a blurry image.

4. **To achieve balanced exposure.** There will be situations in which both the aperture and ISO values are predetermined and achieving proper exposure can only be accomplished by adjusting the shutter speed.

ISO

ISO is a little more difficult to explain because there are no mechanical analogies that really help; but I know you can handle it.

As we discussed earlier, digital camera sensors contain millions of pixels. Each pixel produces an electric signal representing the color and intensity of the light to which it's exposed. The camera's electronics record the signals produced by the pixels.

When a lot of light hits the sensor, the camera's electronics receive a good, strong signal from the pixels and can record it with no modification. However, when light levels are low, the pixel's output signals are also low, and the camera needs to amplify them in order to record them effectively. (**Note:** *Think of this as turning up the gain on a microphone.*) But when the low-level signal is amplified, the self-noise of the camera's electronics is also amplified. In an audio device, this noise would sound like a hiss. In a video camera, it appears as visible grains or blotches.

While modern cameras can capture relatively clean images at higher ISOs, it's almost always desirable to keep your ISO value as low as possible when recording video. The most common reason to increase ISO is when your aperture is at its widest, your shutter speed is at its lowest (without camera shake becoming an issue), and you have no choice but to raise your ISO to achieve proper exposure.

The Exposure Triangle

If you think back to middle school geometry, you'll recall the sum of the angles of any triangle always equal 180 degrees. If you change one of the angles, one or both of the remaining angles has to change in order to maintain the 180-degree sum.

If you think about camera exposure as a triangle, aperture, shutter speed, and ISO would each be one of the three angles. In this comparison, *proper exposure* would be equivalent to the triangle's *180-degree rule*. Any time a change is made to one of the exposure parameters—either for creative or technical reasons—one or both of the remaining parameters must be adjusted to keep the exposure balanced. Here are some examples:

1. **You close the aperture to increase the depth of field.** This situation comes into play when you

want both the foreground and background in focus. To maintain proper exposure, you'd also need to slow your shutter speed (which can create blur in moving objects), or increase the ISO (which increases noise in the image.)

2. **You decrease the shutter speed to smooth out a waterfall.** To keep your exposure balanced, you'd also need to close your aperture which would increase your depth of field. This forces more of your image to be in focus—which may not produce your intended result.

3. **You increase the shutter speed to prevent camera shake at dusk.** Because you're shooting on a smartphone with a fixed aperture, you have no choice but to increase the ISO value and introduce noise to the image.

There are advanced tools and techniques that can deal with some these situations but we won't cover them in this book. The point of these examples is to illustrate how aperture, shutter speed and ISO work together to achieve proper, balanced exposure.

FRAME RATE

This term refers to the number of still images a video camera captures per second. Most consumer-level video cameras (and most smartphones) default to a frame rate of 30p (progressive frames per second). Some will go as high as 60p often at a reduced resolution. And some will optionally record at 24p. We'll discuss 24p in more detail in a moment.

There's sometimes confusion between frame rate and shutter speed. Just remember, frame rate is the number of video images recorded per second while shutter speed is how long the shutter remains open during each captured video image.

24 Frames Per Second

24fps is the frame rate at which most major Hollywood movies and television productions have been filmed for almost a century. Most of us have grown up being familiar with how 24fps film and video looks without ever knowing the definition of *frame rate*.

In 1926 when the first *Talkie* movies were created, film was expensive to produce, develop and transport. 24fps was chosen as a movie industry standard because it was the lowest frame rate that could also support simultaneous sound. That's it. 24fps is still around today because Hollywood movie studios were cost conscious in the 1920s.

What's interesting is that because 24fps has been around for almost 100 years, if you play the same video image to an audience today at two different frame rates—24fps and 30fps—more often than not, the audience will perceive the 24fps version as being more professional and having higher production value. It's difficult to say exactly why this is the case, but I'd speculate that it's because al-most every professional production they've ever seen (other than sporting events) has been shot in 24p.

One of the reasons home video has a *home-video-look* is that it's usually recorded at a frame rate of 30p. Because more video frames are being captured per second, 30p can appear crisper and cleaner than 24p. You might as-sume that *crisper and cleaner* would be preferred by film and video audiences but that's generally not the case.

It's by no means a requirement that you record video at 24p but the fact that audiences associate it with profes-sional productions is a strong incentive. If your camera is capable of shooting 24p, give it a try. I think you'll like the results. But, if your camera doesn't have this ability, don't sweat it. At the end of the day, frame rate is nothing more than an aesthetic issue. Capturing your message on video in a clear and professional manner will always be more important than frame rate.

WHITE BALANCE

I'm almost one hundred percent certain there's been an occasion in the recent past when you've taken a photo, looked at the result and thought to yourself, *"Why does everything look so yellow?"* Not all photos are too yellow. Sometimes they're too blue. And sometimes the color is perfect. Whatever the color, this phenomenon is a result of your camera's *white balance*.

Different light sources have different color tints. Tungsten light bulbs (the kind we've historically used in our homes) have a yellow tint. Newer, energy-efficient compact fluorescent and LED bulbs often have a bluish tint. Midday sun is also bluish. Dawn and dusk sun tends toward yellow and orange.

These tints and hues get added to all the colors in our visual field. Human brains are fairly talented at adjusting what we see so we don't notice the yellow, orange or bluish tints. Digital camera brains aren't as talented. They don't know the color of the light source unless you explicitly tell them.

> **Note:** *Most cameras have an auto white balance setting that makes decent decisions when the lighting in a scene is all the same color. But auto white balance can get confused any time your video frame contains light sources of two or more different colors. And when your camera gets confused, your video ends up looking too yellow or too blue.*

When you set your camera's white balance explicitly (and correctly), whites look white and nothing has an unnatural tint. Getting white balance wrong in your camera isn't the end of the world. Most capable video editing software allows you to adjust the balance after the fact. But your workflow is simplified when you get it right in-camera.

MY RECOMMENDATION

As a reminder, the intention of this book is to help entrepreneurs with no prior video experience get started. In keeping with that intention, my advice is going to consistently push you in the direction of gear you either own or have access to.

If you look around the streets, coffee shops and public buses and trains of the nation, you'll notice almost everyone has some form of smartphone. While we don't always appreciate them, these devices are true marvels. Not only do they make boring ol' phone calls, but they also allow us to send and receive text messages, browse the web, get weather forecasts, perform banking transactions, play games, type notes, take photographs, and record voice memos. And that list just scratches the surface.

It may not surprise you to know that today's smartphones are far more powerful than computers were 50 years ago. But it's absolutely amazing (to me at least) that the tiny devices we now carry around in our pockets and handbags used to take up entire floors of buildings and require multiple PhD-level experts to make them accomplish even the simplest tasks.

Because they're so small and so capable-of-everything, it's easy to forget our smartphones contain high-definition video cameras. And not toy cameras either. In case you're not aware, there have been several feature length films shot either entirely or in part on Apple iPhones. One of them—the documentary *Searching for Sugar Man*—even won an Academy Award.

And while it's unlikely that iOS or Android smartphones will ever take over the Hollywood film industry, it's good to know your pocket-sized mobile device is more than capable of creating Oscar-worthy video footage. This fact alone should convince you that your smartphone has what it takes to create short video clips for your business.

That was a long introduction to my recommendation, which is this:

If you own or have access to an iOS or Android smartphone, use it. Better cameras do exist. But to create compelling, high-quality video for your business, everything you need is literally in your pocket. There's no need to buy anything else.

If you happen to be one of the few people in the world who doesn't currently own a smartphone and has neither the desire nor budget to own one (let's face it, those monthly cellular fees aren't cheap) there may still be a solution for you...

APPLE IPOD TOUCH

This clever little device has almost all the features of an iPhone but: a) has a much lower price tag; and b) doesn't require cellular service.

I won't quote prices in this book, because they tend to change both frequently and dramatically. But it's safe to say you can pick up one of these little treasures for close to USD $200. Then you'll have a very capable high-definition video camera—not to mention all the other Apple iOS goodies—at your fingertips. Here's a link:

Apple iPod Touch

http://davidpower.com/ipodtouch

IMPORTANT NOTE

Any time you use a mobile device (including the iPod Touch) to shoot video, I highly encourage two things:

1. **Close all other apps.** Apps consume memory and processing power. The fewer apps you have open, the more system resources will be available to your video and audio recording apps.

2. **Turn Airplane Mode on.** I advise this for two reasons: a) to prevent your recording from being interrupted by an incoming phone call or text message; and b) to prevent *electromagnetic interference* (EMI) from creating buzzes, hisses, or other distracting noises in your recording.

ONE MORE OPTION

If money is really tight and you're not in the position to own a smartphone or an iPod Touch right now, there's one more option you might want to consider. It's the Logitech C920 webcam.

The C920 is a very popular product. It has a 4.5 out of 5-star rating on over 6,000 Amazon.com reviews. It can capture full, high-definition (1920x1080) video. It attaches to a tripod without fancy adapters. It's a USB device that's compatible with both Mac and Windows PCs. It comes with software that allows you not only to adjust various camera parameters (including resolution, exposure, focus, white balance and more), but also to record video conveniently to your computer's hard drive. Best of all, the C920 costs well under USD $100—much less if you grab it during a sale. Here's a link:

Logitech C920 Webcam

http://davidpower.com/c920

There's no doubt the Logitech C920 is a great, low-cost alternative to a smartphone. However, there are two factors to consider before marching down the webcam path.

1. **A webcam has to be connected to a computer.** This somewhat limits your flexibility. Unlike a smartphone or iPod Touch, a webcam has to be connected to a USB port on a computer in order to record video. If you'll normally shoot in a single indoor location, this won't be much of a limitation for you. It's fairly easy to connect a webcam to a laptop or desktop computer and shoot as much and as often as you'd like. But if you want to shoot at a remote location, either indoors or outdoors, you'll need to lug a laptop with you. While that's

not the end of the world, it is something you'll want to be aware of and plan for.

2. **You'll have to record audio on a second device.** This point will make more sense after you've read the chapter on *Microphones.* The short explanation is that a webcam's built-in microphone is too small and too far away from your mouth to capture high-quality audio. In order for a webcam to be a viable camera alternative, you'll need to capture audio on a lavalier microphone. The microphone I recommend in the next chapter is designed to be used with an iOS or Android smartphone—not a webcam. Normally, this is where I'd recommend a USB lavalier microphone—one that plugs into your computer and allows you to record audio at the same time you're capturing video. The problem is, I haven't yet found one that produces acceptable results at a reasonable price. The only recommendations I can offer at this time are significantly more expensive. And once you'd purchased the C920 webcam, plus the more expensive microphone, plus the accessories you need for it, you'd have spent very close to the cost of an iPod Touch. Maybe even more.

This may seem like a very long-winded way of talking you out of buying a C920 webcam, but that's not the case. The C920 is a great device, and it is a viable alternative to a smartphone provided you have both: a) a way to record high-quality audio separately; and b) the skills necessary to synchronize audio and video later during the editing process.

Microphones

ONE OF THE MOST common and most distracting problems I see in videos created by new entrepreneurs is...

You guessed it.

Bad audio.

Even if your script, performance, and video image are perfect in every way, you can absolutely ruin an otherwise amazing video if your audio quality is poor.

What makes audio poor?

Here are several things in no particular order:

1. **Relying on the microphone built into your camera.** A built-in microphone of any type will not produce acceptable audio; it can't. It's the size of the head of a pin. And it's typically six to ten feet away from you. In order to capture high-quality

audio, you need a dedicated microphone. You won't need to spend thousands of dollars, but you will need to make a small-ish investment.

2. **Recording in a small, empty room with lots of bare walls.** When you speak (or make a sound of any type) in any room, sound waves bounce off of the walls, ceiling, and floor and back to your microphone. Empty rooms are the worst because the bounces themselves bounce around the room several times before they run out of energy. Your microphone records this series of bounces (known as *reverb*) and this makes your words difficult to understand. Worse yet, when it's extreme, room reverb makes your audio sound unprofessional. And we want to avoid *unprofessional* at all costs.

3. **Being too far away from the microphone.** It doesn't matter what type of microphone you're using, or how much you paid for it, your audio will always, always, always sound better the closer it is to your mouth. It is possible to overdo this advice—if your lips are touching the microphone, you're probably too close. For most microphones, four to six inches is a good target distance.

4. **Using the wrong type of microphone.** Microphones are tools. But not every tool is a good fit for every job. For example, you wouldn't (in fact, *couldn't*) use a Phillips screwdriver to tighten a Robertson screw. In much the same way, the

right type of microphone will depend on where you record, and the type of video you're making. The microphone I'll recommend for a live action video is very different than the one I'll recommend for a screencast.

5. **Not using the microphone properly.** Sticking with the tool analogy, if you attempt to tighten a screw by holding the metal shaft and turning the screwdriver's handle against the screw, you're not going to be happy with the result; trust me. You probably wouldn't make such an extreme error with a microphone (I hope). But there are a few simple techniques you can use to dramatically improve the quality of your recordings and we'll cover those later in the book.

Despite these precautions and guidelines, microphones aren't complicated devices. At a very basic level they convert sound waves into electrical signals that ultimately get stored in digital format to your smartphone, computer hard drive or memory card. Next, let's discuss what I recommend.

MY RECOMMENDATION

I have two microphone recommendations and they depend largely on the type of video you're making.

LIVE ACTION MICROPHONE

When you're live in front of a camera, you generally don't want a microphone blocking a huge portion of your face and torso. So unless you're a podcaster and the *microphone-in-your-face* look is an integral part of your brand image, a big, broadcast-style microphone is likely to be distracting to your viewers.

For this reason, microphones used in live action shoots are typically hidden. There are several ways to hide a microphone in this type of shoot but the least expensive and least complex (in terms of setup, placement and overall usage) is the *lavalier* microphone.

The lavalier or *lapel* microphone is a small condenser microphone that can be clipped to a shirt, blouse, jacket or tie. When necessary, it can even be hidden beneath clothing, in hair, under a hat, or attached to eyeglasses. Recording engineers can be very creative when they need to be.

Lavalier mics have what's known as an omni-directional pickup pattern. This means they're equally sensitive to sounds to the front, rear and sides of the microphone's diaphragm. If this sounds like a negative, it really isn't. Lavaliers are typically mounted within six or so inches of your mouth so they require less preamplifier gain and therefore pick up less of the noises you don't want to record. Also, the fact that they hear equally well in all directions means you don't need to be an expert audio engineer to produce good results. You can clip a lavalier mic pretty much anywhere on your upper torso and you're good to go.

For a newbie video creator, the lavalier mic is a good choice because:

1. You can purchase a high-quality lavalier at a reasonable price.

2. It doesn't require any additional mounting hardware. As long as you're wearing clothing, you're in good shape.

3. The omni-directional pickup pattern makes it very easy to place and orient.

The model I recommend to newbies is the RODE SmartLav+. It's designed to plug directly into either an iOS or Android phone or tablet. RODE even offers a free iOS app that can get you up and running quickly.

RODE SmartLav+

http://davidpower.com/smartlavp

One more detail: The cable on this microphone is fairly short—just under 4 feet long. So if you plan to record video and audio simultaneously on a single smartphone, you'll need RODE's extension cable available here:

RODE SmartLav+ Extension

http://davidpower.com/lavextension

SCREENCAST MICROPHONE

When you record your voice for a tutorial, online course module, screen share, video sales letter, or any other video in which your face doesn't appear on camera, you have a few more microphone options:

1. If you're going to appear in live action videos and have already invested in a SmartLav+ microphone, use this same microphone for voice overs in your screencast videos. There's little point in buying a second microphone if the one you own will get the job done nicely. As always, position the microphone as close as you can to your mouth and ensure the room you record in doesn't generate too much reverb.

   There's an added benefit to using the same microphone for both live action and voice over purposes. It's not uncommon for an online course (or similar educational content) to contain both live action and screencast segments. If you use the same microphone, and record all segments in the same room with the same preamplifier settings, your voice will sound consistent throughout the entire video. Major bonus.

2. If your budget permits owning two microphones *or* screencast-style videos will be the sole focus of your business promotion efforts, you may want to consider a dynamic microphone.

Dynamic microphones are the type typically used by radio broadcasters and podcasters. The main benefit of a dynamic mic is that it's sensitive only to sounds immediately in front of it. Sounds you don't want your audience to hear—things like air conditioning, computer fans, keyboard presses, and mouse clicks—are almost silent. As you might suspect, dynamic microphones are also less sensitive to room reverb so they do a great job in rooms that don't sound so great on their own.

I hope I've already convinced you the SmartLav+ is an excellent microphone for recording to an iOS or Android smartphone. But when you create screencast videos, it's often convenient to record audio directly to your computer. Unfortunately, the SmartLav+ isn't able to do this without some elaborate modification.

Thankfully, there's another, not-so-expensive option: the Audio-Technica ATR2100. This is a dynamic microphone that connects directly to either a Windows or Mac computer via USB, and gets you up and running with little to no fuss. The ATR2100 comes boxed with all the cables you need in order to connect it. You'll need a couple of inexpensive accessories to make it perform at its best and we'll cover those in the *Accessories* chapter. Here's a link to the ATR2100:

Audio-Technica ATR2100

http://davidpower.com/atr2100

BUT I ALREADY OWN A CONDENSER MICROPHONE!

A lot of the complaints I've heard from (and about) novice video creators stems from the fact that they've bought an inexpensive USB condenser microphone, placed it on their desk three or four feet away, cranked the gain way up, and started recording. This results in a fairly equal mix of the narrator's voice plus:

- Their computer fan

- Their keyboard and mouse clicks

- Their air conditioner

- Traffic noise

- A neighbor mowing their lawn

- Room reverb

If you happen to be someone who accepted questionable advice from a novice video creator and you're now stuck with a cheap condenser microphone that isn't producing great results, don't worry. There's still hope. You don't have to trash your microphone and buy a new one. Here are a few simple techniques you can use to make huge improvements in your audio recordings without spending another dime:

1. **Move the microphone closer to your mouth.** The further a microphone is away from

your mouth, the more noise it picks up. When recording voice over for a screencast, position the microphone within four to six inches of your mouth and ensure you maintain that distance throughout your entire narration.

2. **Always use a pop filter.** One of the biggest rookie audio mistakes is recording excessive *plosives*. These are 'P', 'B' and 'T' sounds that create loud, distracting distortion on your audio recordings. You can get rid of plosives once and for all with a $10 pop filter. This solution is so cheap, there's no excuse for not owning one. Just make sure you use it every time you record. (**Note:** You'll get much better results with a nylon mesh pop filter than you will with a foam windscreen. See the *Accessories* chapter for recommendations.)

3. **Reduce the gain on your preamplifier.** Whether or not you're aware of it, your microphone will always have some form of preamplifier. For a USB microphone, the preamp is built into the microphone body. If you're a little more advanced, your microphone may be plugged into an external audio interface or mixer. No matter what gear you're using, *high gain* equals *high noise*. Always keep your gain as low as possible while still maintaining a strong signal. How do you gauge the strength of the signal? Your interface, recorder, or recording software will almost always have a meter that

dances around as you speak into your microphone. A strong signal will average around two thirds of the meter's length or height while you're speaking at a normal volume. At all costs, avoid the input signal hitting the very top of the meter. This means the signal has clipped. Clipping sounds terrible, and it's almost impossible to fix after the fact. If you're dealing with a low signal, your first solution should be moving closer to the microphone. Once you're as close as you can comfortably be, increase the gain slowly until your meter averages around the two thirds level while you're speaking.

While these guidelines aren't silver bullets, if you follow them closely on your next voice over recording, you'll improve the quality of your audio by a huge margin. You're welcome.

[6]

Audio Recorders

I F YOU'VE FOLLOWED my advice so far, you'll be shoot-ing your first few videos with your smartphone and re-cording audio simultaneously with a SmartLav+. The good news is, with a little practice and patience, your videos are going to be great!

The other good news is that by recording audio and video at the same time on the same mobile device, your produc-tion workflow is going to be very straightforward. Video clips will come directly out of your phone with audio al-ready embedded and you won't have to spend additional time synchronizing audio and video files from two differ-ent sources.

But you might at some point find yourself in a situation where you're not able to record audio and video on the same device. This might happen if you need to stand fur-ther away from the camera than a microphone extension cable will reach. It might also be necessary if you're demonstrating a physical activity (a dance move or exercise routine, for instance) where a microphone cable would be inconvenient or potentially dangerous.

What can you do in in these situations?

One solution is to invest in a wireless microphone kit. But even a low-end wireless kit is on the expensive side and because you're new to video creation, I don't recommend the added expense or complexity until you've gained more experience.

For right now, the solution is much, much simpler...

USE A SECOND SMARTPHONE

Recording audio on a second device is common in the film industry where it's known as *double-system recording*. All you need to do is beg, borrow or steal (but I don't recommend stealing) a second iOS or Android mobile device and follow this process:

1. Connect your SmartLav+ microphone to the first smartphone.

2. Adjust the gain accordingly.

3. Start your audio recording app.

4. Hide the microphone cable and smartphone beneath your clothing.

5. Start your video recording app on the second smartphone.

6. Look directly at the camera and make one *big, loud handclap* in front of your face.

7. Start performing.

The "big, loud hand clap" is what's note as a *slate marker*. You'll use this to synchronize your audio and video tracks later when you're editing the footage. You'll find a detailed tutorial on how this is done at the following link:

Audio / Video Synchronization Tutorial

http://davidpower.com/avsync

The only real downside of this *hidden recorder* method is that it's not possible for you to monitor the recording in real time. This means that if a problem occurs—the phone's battery dies, the phone runs out of memory, the microphone gain is too high or too low—you won't know about it while you're performing. You'll have to wait until your performance is complete and play back your recording to discover the problem. And at that point, it's too late to do anything about it other than repeat the performance from the beginning.

The caution here is to always check batteries, memory and gain settings before you begin recording. If you follow this guideline, you can avoid most of these problems most of the time.

MY RECOMMENDATION

Whenever and wherever possible, record audio and video simultaneously to the same smart device. It simplifies both the expense and complexity of your shoot and the subsequent editing of the footage.

However, when you encounter a situation in which a single device shoot isn't possible, don't be intimidated by double-system recording. It isn't difficult as long as you take the necessary precautions regarding charging, memory and gain, and use a *big, loud hand clap* to slate the scene.

[7]

Lighting

LIGHTING CAN BE a complex topic. However, for the purposes of this book, we'll keep it very simple.

> *Note: For any kind of screencast video consisting of slides and/or screen captures, lighting won't be an issue. It's only when your face appears on screen that exposure and lighting become important.*

First things first, any time a human face appears in a live action video (and that will be most of the time for us entrepreneurs), our primary lighting goal will be to ensure the face is properly exposed. That's not to say we'll completely ignore other elements of the video frame but if we have to set priorities, our face will always be number one on the list.

Professional lighting kits can be expensive and complex to set up and use. Once you gain more experience, purchasing an economical lighting kit is a logical next step and a good investment. But for right now, let's discuss ways you can produce good results while keeping your budget and the complexity of your setup at reasonable levels.

SHOOTING OUTDOORS

Natural sunlight has a number of advantages for us video-creators-on-budgets:

1. **It's free.** Until someone figures out a way to charge for sunlight (and I'm certain someone somewhere is working on that), it doesn't cost us a dime to use natural light to illuminate our videos.

2. **It's big, bright and everywhere.** Not having to carry, set up, and adjust lighting gear simplifies almost any shoot. The fact that the sun is available everywhere on earth for at least part of the day means when you use natural daylight properly, you always have access to a brilliant light source.

CHALLENGES

While there are a lot of reasons to love the sun (many of them not related to video), you should be aware that direct sunlight presents several challenges to a video creator:

1. **It's almost impossible to control.** The fact that the sun is so big and so bright makes it close to im-

possible for us mere mortals to control. Hollywood does a fairly good job controlling the sun with huge, heavy diffusers and scrims. But these are expensive and require teams of people to construct and position. These types of solutions aren't typically feasible for entrepreneurs like you and me.

2. **It creates harsh shadows.** When you're in open sunlight, facial features (your nose, chin, and the ridges over your eyes) create harsh, unappealing and distracting shadows on your face and neck.

3. **It changes over time.** As the sun moves across the sky, shadows change in shape and direction. If you have to edit together multiple takes filmed over the course of several hours, these changes can be noticeable and distracting to your audience. It's also the case that sunlight changes color very quickly in the early morning and late evening. So adjusting your camera's white balance can be challenging at those times of day.

Solutions

If your business is in the health, exercise, gardening, or ecology niches (for example) and shooting outdoors is important to your brand or message, here are a few pointers that will help you produce the best results:

1. **Shoot in open shade.** Simply put, get out of direct sunlight. Put an awning, a tree, a building, or some

other large shadow-making structure between you and the sun. At the same time, it's important to ensure there's enough ambient light to expose your face properly.

2. **Shoot on an overcast day.** Relying on weather for a successful shoot is never ideal. But a good cloud cover diffuses sunlight and softens otherwise harsh facial shadows.

3. **Shoot at dawn or dusk.** The sun's light is softer and more pleasing in both color and intensity shortly after it rises and shortly before it sets. If you need to shoot outdoors, dawn and dusk are good choices provided you can complete the shoot fairly quickly. (***Note:*** *It's worth keeping in mind that shadows are at their longest at these times of day, so that may put constraints on the placement of both your camera and subject.*)

4. **Use a reflector.** Even in open shade or under overcast skies, you'll encounter situations where facial shadows are more noticeable than you'd prefer. Provided you have a shooting partner to hold it, you can use a reflector or a *white bounce card* to reflect natural light onto your subject's face to soften shadows or remove them completely.

5. **Shoot quickly.** Even if you follow all the advice in this section, it's still a good idea to shoot as quickly

as you can. At the risk of hitting this note too hard: the sun's light changes in position, intensity, and color as it moves across the sky. The more quickly you shoot, the less noticeable these changes will be to viewers of your final, produced video.

Note: In addition to light control, one other difficulty you'll encounter when shooting outdoors is noise. Unless you shoot in a quiet area where there are no cars, lawn mowers, or kids playing, these noises are going to be audible on your video. Even if the environment is quiet, your SmartLav+ microphone is very sensitive to wind so even slight breezes can ruin a take. I'm not trying to talk you out of shooting outdoors. I just want you to be aware of the challenges you might encounter when you do.

SHOOTING INDOORS

You almost always have better control over lighting when you shoot indoors. Here are two different methods to consider:

NATURAL LIGHT

When shooting indoors using nothing but natural light, my advice is the same as when you shoot outdoors: Avoid direct sunlight. If at all possible, use a north facing window to illuminate your subject's face and shoot as quickly as you feasibly can to avoid dramatic shifts in the sun's position, color, and intensity.

ARTIFICIAL LIGHT

When shooting indoors with artificial light, it's a good idea—particularly if you need to shoot over the course of several hours—to completely block all natural light out of the room. You can do this by closing drapes, curtains or shades, or by hanging blankets over exterior windows (assuming the blankets are not visible in the video frame).

When you block out natural light, you have full control over every aspect of the lighting in your scene. The look of your video is in no way influenced by the position, intensity, or color of natural sunlight. This means you can take as much time as you need without worrying about factors that are outside of your control.

The other good news is that, with a little planning and attention to detail, you can produce great results using only the lights already sitting around your home, office, or other indoor shoot location. The next section covers the basics.

THE WORLD'S SHORTEST THREE-POINT LIGHTING TUTORIAL

The *three-point* system is an industry standard when it comes to photography, film and video lighting. It consists of using three distinct light sources to illuminate your subject: a *key* light, a *fill* light, and a *hair* light. On a professional video set, these would often be large lights on separate stands with dimmers and trained lighting specialists to set them up, position them, and control their intensity.

In the down-and-dirty, on-the-cheap tutorial that follows, we're going to keep it simple and use only the lights you have available around your home or office.

> **Note:** *In the movie business, the ceiling and table light fixtures in your home are known as practical lights or just practicals for short.*

1. Place your subject directly below a ceiling fixture. This throws light on the top of the subject's head and across their shoulders. This helps focus the viewer's attention by separating the subject from the background. If it's possible to dim this light to the point at which it's just subtly visible, that's ideal.

2. Place table lamps with shades at similar distances on both the left and right side of the subject (i.e. two lamps in total). Position these as closely as you can to your subject without them being visible in the camera's viewfinder.

3. If possible, dim one of the table lamps so it's slightly less bright than the other. This creates soft shadows on one side of the face and gives the subject more visual depth. (**Note:** With a female subject, you'll want to ensure any shadows you create are very, very subtle.)

Note: *The brighter of the two table lamps is known as the key light. The other is the fill light. You've likely deduced the ceiling fixture described in bullet #1 is the hair light.*

Once you've set up your lights and you're happy with the way the subject appears, adjust your camera's ISO setting so your subject's face is properly exposed. Then start shooting.

MY RECOMMENDATION

As with most of the advice I'll offer in this book, I recommend using gear you either own or have access to rather than spending money on *more stuff*. If you follow the guidelines in this chapter, you'll be able to produce consistently good results shooting both indoors and outdoors without additional gear.

However, there will be times when you'll want to either modify or augment available light in order to create a look you're happy with. Here are a couple of inexpensive components that will help:

REFLECTOR

As discussed earlier in the chapter, it's often helpful to use a reflector to bounce light onto your subject's face to remove shadows and/or achieve proper exposure. Here's an inexpensive model that's 43 inches in diameter and collapses down to just over 12 inches for storage.

Collapsible Reflector

http://davidpower.com/reflector

What's that? A collapsible reflector's not in the budget right now? No problem. Make a trip to your local art supply store and pick up a large sheet (i.e. at least 24" x 36") of white foam core board. It won't fold up nicely like a collapsible reflector but it reflects light equally as well and at a much lower price point.

MINI-LED LIGHT

If your budget permits, a small, dimmable, battery-powered LED light is extremely versatile pretty much anywhere you shoot. You can use it outdoors to remove facial shadows. You can use it indoors as a key, fill, or hair light depending on where you need it. Best of all, there are a ton of inexpensive models available.

Here's one of the most highly-rated options at its price point. It's dimmable, can be powered by AA batteries, and comes with both a diffuser (to soften its intensity) and a *Color Temperature Orange* (CTO) filter (to match the color of practical lights in most homes). Just remember, if you buy a light, you'll need either a small stand or a partner to hold it while you shoot.

LED Light Panel

http://davidpower.com/miniled

If you're interested in learning more about lighting, I offer a ***Lighting For Video Mini-Course*** and I welcome you to enroll for ***free*** at the following link:

Lighting For Video Mini-Course

http://davidpower.com/lighting-course

[8]

Accessories

I N THE STRICTEST SENSE, *accessories* tend to be optional items that aren't absolutely necessary. However,
the components I discuss in this chapter are what I
call *must-have accessories*. Under most circumstances,
they're not optional. You absolutely need these things in
order to capture high-quality video and audio.

The good news is that you won't have to spend a ton of
money. I've done the research, purchased and used these
items myself and I'm happy to share the exact components I consider to be the best balance between price and
quality.

TRIPOD

A tripod isn't a complicated piece of gear but it's surprisingly one of the most overlooked components of a camera
kit. There are people who buy a bunch of video gear, set it
all up, and then ask a partner to hold their camera while

they record. Then of course, their video looks shaky, distracting, and unprofessional. Don't be one of those people.

A solid tripod is a good investment. It keeps your video rock steady. It protects your camera by reducing the possibility of it being dropped and damaged. And perhaps best of all, a tripod lets you work alone on those occasions when you don't have a partner around to help.

You might be tempted to buy a mini-tripod—the type you need to lay on a table or desk in order to film at eye level—but I recommend a full-height model (one that reaches a height of at least 60 inches) so you can film most adults at eye level when standing without having to rely on other furniture.

MY RECOMMENDATION

This is an affordable 60" tripod that collapses down to 20" for storage. It's lightweight, has a three-way head, two bubble levels, and comes with a travel bag. Hard to beat for the price.

Tripod

http://davidpower.com/tripod

TRIPOD MOUNT

Tripods are designed to connect to cameras. But smartphones aren't cameras. Are you confused yet?

Consumer-level tripod heads have what are known as 1/4"-20 threads designed to screw into a 1/4"-20 hole in the bottom of a video or still camera. Unless you have a very special smartphone, it won't have anything close to a 1/4"-20 hole in it. If it does, you've got a huge problem on your hands.

Fear not; all is not lost. Given how popular smartphone photography and video has become in recent years, a number of companies now make accessories that adapt your smartphone to the 1/4"-20 standard.

These adapters, often referred to as *smartphone tripod mounts*, accomplish two important goals:

1. They grip your phone securely without scratching it.

2. They attach to the standard mounting hardware on your tripod.

There are a lot of affordable models available but I recommend staying away from the super-cheap ones. A quality smartphone-to-tripod adapter costs only a little more. Plus, it will last longer and keep your phone safer.

MY RECOMMENDATION

This tripod mount is adjustable, connects to any standard tripod, and is all metal construction. It even has rubber pads to prevent your smartphone from getting scratched. The model I link to below comes with an expansion kit in case you ever need to mount a plus-size smartphone.

Tripod Mount

http://davidpower.com/tripodmount

POP FILTER

Pop filters have one and only one function: to prevent plosives from reaching your microphone. Plosives are the sharp bursts of air your mouth produces when you make 'P', 'B', and sometimes 'T' sounds. There's nothing good about plosives. They're very loud, very distracting, and they make your audio sound very unprofessional.

If you're using a lavalier microphone (such as the SmartLav+), you won't need a pop filter. Mounted to your clothing just below your chin the SmartLav+ typically doesn't pick up plosives. It also comes with a removable foam windscreen that reduces breath noises that do happen to reach it.

However, if you own a microphone such as the Audio-Technica ATR2100 and you use it at the recommended distance and position (i.e. within four to six inches directly in front of your mouth), you absolutely need a pop filter to control plosives.

A pop filter is inexpensive and it's the single-most effective way to remove plosive problems from your audio recordings once and for all.

My Recommendation

I use this model almost every day. It has two layers of nylon mesh, attaches to pretty much any microphone stand, and is easily adjustable to almost any imaginable angle. Also, it's super-inexpensive.

Pop Filter

http://davidpower.com/popfilter

Note: *Foam windscreens that fit over the top of your microphone might be a little less expensive but they're not as effective. For the best value, I absolutely recommend the nylon mesh style linked above.*

Microphone Stand

Again here, you'll only need a stand if you're using a broadcast-style microphone like the ATR2100. You *can* hold a microphone in your hand, but I don't recommend it. Every time you shift your hand on the microphone body, the *handling noise* will be audible on your recording. That creates more trouble than it's worth. An inexpensive desktop stand keeps your hands off the microphone and allows you to read from your computer screen while you're narrating voice overs. Money well-spent.

MY RECOMMENDATION

Here's a desktop microphone stand I personally own and use regularly for narration work at my desk. It's sturdy, height-adjustable, and affordable.

Desktop Mic Stand

http://davidpower.com/deskmicstand

Section Three

Software

[9]

DAW Software

Note: DAW is an acronym for Digital Audio Work-station. While the options we discuss in this chapter aren't full-featured, professional versions, they're close enough to deserve the DAW label.

I F YOU FOLLOW my advice to the letter, you'll be recording audio and video to your smartphone at the same using the same app. As we've discussed, this simplifies both your shooting and editing workflows.

However, there may be times when you want to plug in your Audio-Technica ATR2100 and record audio directly into your computer for use in screencast videos. As your skills and experience improve, you may also encounter situations when you want to be more surgical with audio editing—remove long silences and alternate takes, repair glitches, adjust volume, and perform more advanced processing.

If all of this sounds out of your depth right now, don't sweat it. It won't be long before these terms and techniques are second nature to you. In the meantime, I'm happy to introduce you to a couple of very capable DAW packages that won't cost you a penny. Here they are:

GARAGEBAND (MAC ONLY)

If you own a Mac computer or any kind of iOS device, you're likely familiar with GarageBand. It comes installed on most Apple products, has the familiar Mac look-and-feel, and is capable of most of the audio recording and editing features you'll need at this stage. If you live in the Apple ecosystem, GarageBand is a great option. In the off chance your Mac or iOS device mysteriously doesn't have GarageBand installed, here's a download link:

GarageBand

> *http://davidpower.com/garageband*

AUDACITY (WINDOWS & MAC)

Audacity is available as a free download for both Windows and Mac operating systems. It was designed and built by some very smart professors and graduate students at Carnegie Mellon University in Pittsburgh, PA. At a functional level, Audacity is more advanced than GarageBand but it's a little less user-friendly. The good news is there are a ton of screencast tutorials available online to walk you through the basic functionality. And when you're ready for them, you'll also find advanced tutorials on more complex editing and processing techniques. And these tutorials are only ever a Google search away. Here's the Audacity download link:

Audacity

http://davidpower.com/audacity

MY RECOMMENDATION

Being a long-time audio geek and Windows user, I'm a big fan of Audacity. For a free software package, it surprisingly offers almost everything you'll need as a beginner. Audacity gets my top vote for any new video creator using a Windows PC. I also recommend Audacity to anyone on a Mac system who's outgrown GarageBand.

[10]

Presentation Software

PRESENTATION SOFTWARE IS an indispensable tool to any entrepreneur. You'll find it useful for a number of different purposes including tutorials, online course content, video sales letters, and public talks and presentations.

Not surprisingly, applications are available for both Windows and Mac platforms and the latest versions allow you to:

1. Create and modify files on your mobile device.

2. Record audio narration.

3. Export your presentation as a video.

Here are the current contenders:

KEYNOTE (MAC ONLY)

The desktop version of Keynote is available for purchase and download from the Mac App store at a very reasonable price. Slightly less-capable, free versions are also available for iOS and for web browsers through iCloud.com. Keynote presentations created on the iOS and cloud-based apps can be shared with the desktop version for more advanced editing and processing.

Even Windows PC owners can use the cloud version of Keynote for free if they have an iCloud.com account. So that's a plus. Here's a link to the desktop version of Keynote:

Keynote

http://davidpower.com/keynote

POWERPOINT (WINDOWS & MAC)

PowerPoint has been around for a number of years. It's part of the Microsoft Office suite, and is available for both Windows and Mac computers. It's easy to use and has pretty much all the features you'd want in a presentation package.

The newest version of PowerPoint even has a built-in screen recording feature so you can capture what's happening on your computer screen and embed it into a PowerPoint presentation. That's a major bonus. Here's a link to more information on PowerPoint:

PowerPoint

http://davidpower.com/powerpoint

MY RECOMMENDATION

Because it's available for both Mac and Windows operating systems, PowerPoint is my top pick for presentation software. The fact that you can record audio narration and screen captures directly within PowerPoint, combine them with your slide content and later export the entire presentation to MP4 video format means you can get a lot of mileage out of this one piece of software.

The *Microsoft Office 365 Home* plan lets you install the entire Office package (including Outlook, Excel, Word, Publisher, PowerPoint, OneNote, and Access) on up to five Windows or Mac computers for one low annual fee. That's an absolute deal if you ask me. Here's a link to further details:

Microsoft Office 365 Home

http://davidpower.com/office365

[11]

Screen Capture Software

THERE ARE A NUMBER of screen capture applications available and if you search around, you'll likely find at least a few cheaper options than the two I discuss in this chapter. But you're not likely to find anything offering as many features or flexibility. The two applications we'll discuss here both have best-in-class features including:

1. **High-quality screen capture recording.** Lesser screen capture software often limits the capture resolution and/or frame rate. The applications I recommend are capable of full HD (1920 x 1080) capture at frame rates up to 30 frames per second so they produce videos that are crystal clear and flicker-free.

2. **Elaborate image annotation.** Both packages allow you to add captions, arrows, underlines, blurs, highlights, zooms, pans, sound effects and a host of other embellishments to enhance the clarity

and production value of your screen capture videos.

3. **Video editing.** In addition to plain ol' screen capture, both applications offer full-featured video editors that permit you to cut, copy, paste, insert, click, drag, and reorder multiple audio and video clips on a multi-track timeline. Unless and until you find yourself needing more elaborate video editing features, either of these packages will perform all the basic editing functions you'll require.

4. **Full-featured export.** Both packages offer full control over the resolution and format of your final video. Both also offer the ability to share directly to popular social networks, video hosts and cloud storage platforms including Facebook, YouTube, Vimeo, Google Drive, DropBox and others.

An added benefit of buying into one of the better-known applications is that there are a ton of online forums, tutorials, and walk-throughs that address pretty much any challenge you might encounter. There's strength in numbers.

There's one more big bonus. Because both applications in this category offer full-featured video editing, if you invest in one of them, you won't have to purchase and learn yet another separate editing package. And fewer pieces of software is always a good thing.

With the introduction out of the way, here are my top picks for screen capture software.

SCREENFLOW (MAC ONLY)

ScreenFlow comes at a reasonable price and offers all of the capture and editing goodies we discussed earlier in this chapter. The company is well-known and the software is popular among Mac users. Here's the link:

ScreenFlow

http://davidpower.com/screenflow

CAMTASIA (WINDOWS & MAC)

Everything I've written about ScreenFlow is also true for Camtasia. The company (TechSmith) is reputable and in the Fall of 2016, they revamped the product to add a host of new, advanced features and align their Windows and Mac versions.

Camtasia

http://davidpower.com/camtasia

MY RECOMMENDATION

As a long-time Windows user, I highly recommend Camtasia. It has all the features you'd want in a screen capture package plus an easy-to-use video editor. Its most recent feature enhancements make it possible to create attractive explainer videos and video sales letters. It's not a cheap piece of software but it's also not super-expensive. In my opinion, it's a worthwhile investment for anyone who's serious about making videos for their business. Visit the Camtasia link above and watch the demo videos on the product. They'll give you a good feel for the software's capabilities.

[12]

Video Apps

YOUR FIRST THOUGHT might be, *"My phone has a video app. Why do I need another one?"*

Here's the answer:

Built-in video apps are designed to produce decent results for most people. And most people don't want to spend any time thinking about or adjusting focus, aperture, shutter speed, frame rate, white balance, audio gain, or any other parameter. They just want to pick up their phone, point it at their toddler (or police officer), hit record and get a not-too-terrible-looking video they can share on Facebook three and a half minutes later. In Apple-speak, they want their video app to just work.

Built-in camera apps are designed for *that* type of user, not for entrepreneurs like you and I. We aren't satisfied with *not-too-terrible-looking*. We use video to market our products and services to prospective customers, and we need reliable, consistent, and controllable results across a lot of different environments and situations. We simply need more control over the camera's parameters than built-in apps offer us.

Here are the top ways in which built-in, auto-mode smartphone video apps fail us as professional users:

FOCUS

When using a built-in video app, it's not uncommon for your camera to lock onto an object in the frame other than your face. When that happens, your face goes out of focus. It may stay out of focus for several seconds (sometimes longer) until the app decides your face is more important than the bookshelf behind you (for instance) and shifts the focus back. This can happen any number of times during a long video shoot and each time it does, it will distract your viewers. Worse yet, it sends the message, *"This is an amateur production."*

EXPOSURE

In much the same way it makes focus decisions, a built-in app evaluates the amount of light in a scene and adjusts exposure accordingly. But as soon as anything in the scene changes—you move slightly toward or away from the camera, raise your arm, or a cloud momentarily blocks the sun—the app adjusts the camera's exposure parameters to suit the new scene. Visually, everything in the scene jumps from slightly-brighter to slightly-darker and back again as soon as you lower your arm (for instance). Again, this is distracting and sends a not-so-great message to your audience.

Microphone Gain

When doing the magical, mystical, auto-mode thing, a built-in video app constantly evaluates and adjusts the level of the audio its recording. When you speak at a normal level, the app sets a lower microphone gain. But in between words (when the ambient sound level is low), the app boosts the gain in an attempt to keep the entire recording at the same volume. And while its intentions are good, the app ends up amplifying background noise in between words. The resulting recording alternates between clear voice and loud background noise. Again, this is distracting and unprofessional.

White Balance

Built-in video camera apps do their best to set white balance correctly. Yet there are times when they fail miserably. And when they fail, you end up with video footage that's too yellow, too blue or too *something-in-between*. This requires you to spend additional time correcting the camera's error during post-production.

There are other camera parameters we may want to control during a video shoot but focus, exposure, microphone gain, and white balance are the *big-four*. Dedicated video apps take critical decisions away from the camera and give them to the camera user. This means we need to pay closer attention when setting up our smartphones for a shoot but the reward is more consistent, predictable, and professional results.

Here are the top dedicated video apps for both major smartphone platforms:

FiLMiC Pro (iOS & Android)

In addition to full control over all important camera parameters, FiLMiC Pro offers the ability to share and save your videos to Facebook, DropBox, Vimeo, Google Drive and others.

FiLMiC Pro

http://davidpower.com/filmicpro

Cinema FV-5 (Android Only)

Much like FiLMiC Pro, Cinema FV-5 offers full control over advanced camera parameters. It should be your first stop if you're an Android user.

Cinema FV-5

http://davidpower.com/cinemafv5

My Recommendation

While I'm an iPhone user and have experience using FiLMiC Pro, I won't let that bias my recommendation.

Both apps are very strong candidates. If you're an iPhone user, you won't go wrong with FiLMiC Pro.

If you own an Android device, you have choices. I give FiLMiC Pro a slight edge because it offers more flexibility in transferring video files to cloud storage platforms. This makes it easier to get video clips off of your smartphone and onto your desktop computer. In any case, both apps are so inexpensive, you might consider buying both, trying them out and sticking with the one you like best.

> **Note:** *When you visit the links above, be sure to check out the sample films advanced users have made using only their smartphones. I think you'll be impressed.*

[13]

Audio Apps

IF YOU RECORD audio and video simultaneously using your smartphone video app, you won't need a separate audio-only application. I'm including this short chapter so you'll have a reference if you ever need to record audio when or where it's not possible to run a microphone cable.

If your video subject is performing a dance routine, an exercise move or any other physical activity where a microphone cable might be distracting or dangerous, you can attach your SmartLav+ to a second smartphone and carefully hide it out of sight on the subject's body. This second smartphone will run an audio-only app and you'll synchronize the separate audio and video clips later when you edit the footage.

Here are the top options for both major smartphone operating systems:

VOICE RECORD PRO (IOS ONLY)

Voice Record Pro is an impressive app. It's available for free with an in-app purchase to remove small advertisements. It has a lot of advanced configuration options, and the ability to import and export audio to any number of cloud storage platforms including Google Drive, DropBox, OneDrive, iCloud and others.

Voice Record Pro

http://davidpower.com/voicerecordpro

SMART VOICE RECORDER (ANDROID ONLY)

Not being an Android user, I'm at a disadvantage when it comes to recommending Android apps. However, I've researched this and found the top-rated voice recorder app in the Google Play store. Smart Voice Recorder has a 4.4-star rating on over 377,000 reviews. That's an impressive track record. More importantly, the application supports recording in PCM / WAV format which is an absolute must for the type of work we're doing. More on this in the note at the end of this chapter.

Smart Voice Recorder

http://davidpower.com/smartvoice

MY RECOMMENDATION

I've personally used Voice Record Pro for iOS and I'm impressed with its features and performance. But it won't help you at all if you own an Android device. My recommendation here is to stick with the app that's compatible with your flavor of smartphone: Voice Record Pro if you're an iPhone user and Smart Voice Recorder if you're on an Android device.

> **Note**: *Whenever possible, record your audio in WAV format. WAV files are large but this format preserves 100% of the quality of the original. Where possible, I recommend configuring your audio app for a sample rate of 48,000Hz at a bit depth of 24 bits.*

[14]

Video Editing Software

IF YOU PLAN to make any type of live action video for your business, I strongly encourage you to beg, borrow, or steal a video editing package. If you believe you'll ever be able to pull off the perfect performance in a single take and immediately upload it to YouTube with no editing or enhancement, you're kidding yourself. You also might be a little drunk. Editing is where *movie magic* happens. When performed well, editing can transform raw video footage into a compelling, entertaining and professional-looking product.

> **Note:** *I don't recommend editing video on a smartphone or tablet app. These apps may look slick on the surface, but they don't have anywhere close to the level of precise control that a desktop application offers. For that reason, I only recommend desktop software in this chapter.*

Here are some of the more common ways you'll use editing software.

1. **Remove unwanted takes and segments**. When you shoot video, it's not uncommon to let the camera continue to roll between takes. In a situation where your best take was number 3 out of 5, editing software allows you to magically remove takes 1, 2, 4, and 5 and make it look like they never existed. Also, if you shoot alone, your footage will likely contain segments that include you: a) walking from the camera to your mark before you deliver your performance; and b) walking from your mark back to the camera to stop the recording when you're done. Editing software allows you to remove sections of video your audience simply doesn't need (or want) to see.

2. **Add text.** Even the most basic video editing software permits you to add titles, captions and other annotations to your videos.

3. **Add transitions**. Editing software allows you to add fade-ins at the beginnings of your videos and fade-outs at the ends. These simple transitions add a professional polish that's often lacking in amateur productions. (**Note:** Unless you're making a stylized comedy video, never use transitions other than fade-in and fade-out. Anything more elaborate than this screams, *"This is a home video."*)

4. **Add video effects**. It's rare for video footage to come out of your camera looking exactly the way you want. It's equally uncommon for footage shot on different days or under different lighting conditions to look identical. Depending on how, where, and when your video is shot, you may encounter situations where you'll want to add image sharpening, modify white balance, or adjust things like contrast and color saturation. Editing software allows you to make these types of adjustments.

5. **Process audio**. Despite your best intentions, there will be times when you record your audio a little too high, a little too low, or with a little too much noise in the background. Editing software permits you to make volume adjustments, add equalization and compression, and even reduce noise when it's necessary. This ensures your dialog tracks are consistent and intelligible.

This list isn't complete. It's simply a sampling of the more common ways you'll use editing software as a beginner.

If you're not planning to appear on-camera and instead, the sole focus of your video creation efforts will be in the screencast realm (i.e. slides and screen captures with voice over), you *might* be able to get away without owning or using video editing software. But even then, that's a big *might*. I still encourage you to have an editing package handy, and be familiar with how it's used. The more videos you create, the more likely you are to encounter a problem you can only resolve with a quick edit. If you have editing software close at hand, then you'll be prepared and the solution will be quick and painless. And *quick and painless* is how we like to roll.

As always, I'll do my best to keep your budget under control with my recommendations but promise me you'll stay open to the idea of spending at least a little money on a proper video editing software package. Deal? Alright.

As a reminder, if you purchased one of the screen capture applications I recommended in an earlier chapter, you already have both a terrific screen capture system and a very capable video editing package. You're good to go. But if screen capture software isn't in your budget right now, and you need to find a stand-alone editing application, consider starting with one of the following:

iMOVIE (MAC ONLY)

There's nothing too fancy about iMovie. It's reasonably intuitive and allows you to split audio and video clips, move them around, and add basic transitions and effects. If you're a Mac person and you're brand new to video editing, iMovie should be your first stop. If it's not already on your computer, you can download it here for free:

iMovie

http://davidpower.com/imovie

MOVIE MAKER (WINDOWS ONLY)

Much like iMovie, Movie Maker is very straightforward. It allows you to perform most basic audio and video manipulations without overwhelming you with complexity. Movie Maker is available for free download here:

Movie Maker

http://davidpower.com/moviemaker

MY RECOMMENDATION

I recommend you download and evaluate one of the free packages listed above—iMovie if you're a Mac user, and Movie Maker if you're on Windows. Edit and produce at least one entire video using a free application before you invest in paid software. I recommend this because it's difficult to choose the right software package for *you* until *you* are aware of the features you need. Editing for at least a short period using free software will allow you to identify its limitations, and create your own *must-have-features* list that will help you shop intelligently for a paid package.

[15]

Video Hosting

A **VIDEO HOSTING PLATFORM** isn't *software* in the conventional sense. There's generally nothing to download and install on your desktop or mobile device. Hosting platforms are better described as *Software as a Service* (SaaS). That's close enough to warrant including it in the *Software* section of this book.

There are three main players in the video hosting space right now. Here they are in no particular order:

YouTube

I have absolutely no doubt you're familiar with YouTube. There's a better than average chance you've used it (or will use it) at some point today. YouTube is one of the most visited sites on the Internet, and it's free to both consumers and producers of video content. Almost anyone can create a YouTube channel and start uploading videos within minutes.

There are a few noteworthy benefits of hosting your videos on YouTube:

1. **It's free.** It doesn't cost you a penny to create a YouTube channel, upload your videos, embed them in your website, and start sending links out to the world. YouTube has a few reasonable restrictions on the types of content you can upload. Beyond that, the sky's the limit.

2. **It's owned by Google.** You're likely aware that Google is the Internet's number one search engine. The fact that YouTube is owned by Google means the search engine gives priority to YouTube results over all other video hosting platforms. If you're relying on any kind of video SEO (Search Engine Optimization) for people to find your business, Google helps you out tremendously if your videos are available on YouTube.

3. **It's one of the most-visited sites on the Internet.** The fact that millions of people visit YouTube in any given day, *and* that the platform itself is the second most popular search engine in the world means there's a decent chance that people who are interested in your niche will eventually find your content—particularly if it's compelling and well-produced. Even if you opt for a paid video host in the future, it may still make sense to host some of your content on YouTube purely for the free exposure it offers.

If there's a downside to relying solely on YouTube for video hosting, it's the fact that you can't protect your content. While YouTube does permit you to set a video to *Unlisted* status (whereby it doesn't appear in your channel listing or in YouTube searches), I've encountered situations in which unlisted videos appear in Google search results. Also, as soon as one person has the link to an unlisted video, they're free to shared it far and wide across the Internet. There's no reliable way to prevent unauthorized users from accessing your content. This makes YouTube a bad bet for hosting online course videos or any other video content you plan to either charge for or restrict access to.

VIMEO

Vimeo is a great video host with a number of terrific features. They have a free plan that offers a lot of flexibility, and an inexpensive *Plus* plan with even more features, storage space and bandwidth. Unfortunately, both of these plans prohibit you from hosting videos for commercial, for-profit purposes. If you're running a business, Vimeo wants you to upgrade to either their *Pro* or *Business* plans. Both are quite a bit more expensive. These plans are entirely worth the money once your business is generating a decent level of revenue but the cost may be hard to justify in the early stages.

For business owners, the killer feature of Vimeo's more expensive plans is the ability to restrict where your videos can be viewed. For instance, if you run a website called *MyOnlineCourse.com*, you can tell Vimeo to only permit your videos to be played when they're embedded in a web page on *MyOnlineCourse.com*. This prevents people from grabbing a video link and posting it elsewhere on the Internet for others to access.

WISTIA

Wistia is one of the newer players in the video hosting game. In addition to securing your videos to prevent others from copying and sharing them, Wistia has a lot of additional cutting edge features including:

1. **Embedded calls to action.** You can collect email addresses directly within the video player.

2. **Advanced statistics.** Heatmaps show you exactly how viewers have watched, skipped and rewatched various segments of each video.

3. **A customizable player.** Almost every characteristic of the video player can be customized including sizes, colors, controls, captions, social sharing, comments, and more.

4. **Advanced video SEO.** Wistia uses advanced technologies to ensure *your* videos and *your* web pages are given priority over Wistia's website in Internet search results.

This list is just a taste. Wistia's platform is state of the art and they add new features every month.

Wistia offers a free plan that's limited to a total of three videos and a Wistia-branded player. This plan is just enough for you to experiment and decide whether or not the platform is right for you. Unfortunately, their paid plans scale up in price pretty steeply. Unless your business is generating a consistent revenue stream from video, Wistia might be out of your budget at this stage. However, definitely keep them in mind for the future.

MY RECOMMENDATION

I've been a Wistia customer for a couple of years and I continue to be impressed with their platform and the innovative direction they're taking it. Wistia is my top pick for an established business looking for a serious video host. However, as I mentioned above, their paid plans are out of reach for a lot of startups. For that reason, I have a two-step recommendation:

1. When you're starting out, host your videos on YouTube. It's absolutely free and you'll benefit greatly from both the YouTube and Google search strength and popularity. You won't be able to secure your videos, but for any type of marketing, tutorial or sales video, protection usually isn't a concern. The value you'll get from organic SEO far outweighs the lack of protection. Here's the link to YouTube (as if you need it):

YouTube

http://davidpower.com/youtube

2. Once your business is in product creation mode and your video content is generating consistent revenue, I recommend you invest in either a Vimeo or Wistia hosting plan that meets your needs. Vimeo Pro is at the lower end of the scale with Wistia at the higher end. Here are links to both platforms:

Vimeo Pro

http://davidpower.com/vimeopro

Vimeo Business

http://davidpower.com/vimeobusiness

Wistia

http://davidpower.com/wistia

Section Four

Summary

[16]

Conclusion

"The best time to plant a tree was 20 years ago. The second-best time is now."

~ Chinese Proverb

WE'RE VERY CLOSE to the end of this book. But we're at the very start of your video creation journey.

Like most worthwhile endeavors, learning to create compelling, professional videos requires practice, patience, and a reasonable investment of time, energy, and money.

But there is one shortcut you can use to get there quickly.

Wanna know what it is?

Lean in close.

Ready?

Okay, here it is...

START TODAY

I'm absolutely serious. Just as the Chinese proverb above suggests, the best and only shortcut is to start right now.

So, before you go out and buy a single piece of the hardware or software I recommend in this book, here's what I want you to do:

Grab your smartphone, prop it up against a coffee mug and press *Record*. Shoot yourself talking into the lens. Tell your camera what you ate for breakfast, or describe your weekend plans. Tell the same story a few different times in a few different ways. Then pull the video footage off of your camera and play it back on your desktop monitor. Pay close attention to your performance, the lighting, exposure, focus, audio, and all the other nuances of the recording. Choose the best take of the bunch, then edit the file to remove the takes you don't like. Add a short fade-in at the beginning of the video, and a slightly longer fade-out at the end. Go through the process of rendering the video and uploading it to YouTube. Watch it online a couple of times. If you're brave, share it with a few friends who'll give you honest, constructive feedback.

The first video you create will take a long time and probably not look so great. Your second video will be twice as good and take half the time. This improvement in speed and quality will continue each time you make a new video. It won't be long before you review your work and think to yourself, *"Hey, this ain't half bad!"* When you reach that point, you'll know you're ready to release your work; to engage, educate and inspire your audience, and ultimately turn them into consumers of your products and services.

So I'll reiterate the advice above:

Start today!

And as soon as you've created the first piece of video content you're proud of, please drop me an email and share it with me. I'd love to see your work. You'll find my contact details in the *About the Author* section near the end of the book.

THANK YOU

I want to offer a sincere thank-you for reading this book. There are dozens of books available on this topic and you chose to spend your time and attention on mine. I appreciate that.

If you've found this book valuable, I could use your help. Please visit Amazon and take a moment to leave a fair and honest review. Reviews are the most effective way of letting me know you appreciate the content I'm creating. Your honest feedback will help me continue to create books you'll enjoy reading.

Use the following link to leave an Amazon.com review:

http://davidpower.com/evtg-review

Thanks again and best of luck to you.

ABOUT THE AUTHOR

David Power is an author, filmmaker, podcaster, and entrepreneur. In the past decade, he's made close to 100 short films spanning the comedy, music video, documentary, and narrative genres. As host and producer of the Sure-Fire Podcast, David documents the making of an independent comedy feature film called Sure-Fire. David's book Introduction to Podcast Technology is available on Amazon in paperback, Kindle, and Audible formats. When he's not writing, David spends much of his time applying the latest and greatest in digital production techniques across both the audio and video domains. He is also an out-of-the-closet lover of rap music, and incorporates dope rhymes into his educational materials at every opportunity. David lives in Brooklyn, New York with his beautiful wife, Cara.

For more information or to contact David, visit:

http://davidpower.com

Also By David Power

What Podcasting 'Gurus' Don't Tell You

But You Absolutely Must Know Before Starting a Podcast...

One podcasting authority suggests *"Technology isn't important."* Another sums up the entire podcast creation process in a four-minute video. A third insists you can podcast without money, gear or experience. None of them take the time to explain what the buttons, dials and lights all mean—they leave you to figure out the *techie stuff* on your own.

Introduction to Podcast Technology is different. It acknowledges that technology is not the most important aspect of podcasting. However, instead of trying to convince you everything is easy, the book guides you through each stage of the podcast creation process in detail and offers precise, step-by-step instructions on the essential tools and techniques you need to record, produce, and launch a podcast.

Here are just a few of the topics covered in ***Introduction to Podcast Technology***:

- How to tell the difference between a good recording room and a bad one (*and how to avoid wasting time and money when improving a bad room.*)

- **Learn the two main types of microphones and why only one of them is appropriate for most podcasters.**

- Discover the difference between an audio interface and an audio recorder (*and which to choose if you can only afford one or the other.*)

- **Discover the one recording accessory that can make the biggest improvement in the quality of your recordings. (*You'll be surprised how inexpensive this one is.*)**

- How to configure free software (*used by a lot of podcasting pros*) to convert master recordings to MP3 format.

- **Learn what to look for (*and look out for*) when choosing a media host.**

- Discover the most effective method to get your show listed in the iTunes podcast directory.

Book owners also receive **FREE Enrollment** in a 15-day companion video course. Look over the author's shoulder as he breaks down complex podcasting topics including: equalization, compression, MP3 encoding, navigating a media host's dashboard, and more.

Whether you're an aspiring podcaster who's intimidated or overwhelmed by technology, or an experienced professional looking for new production techniques, Introduction to Podcast Technology offers exactly what you need.

Don't let technology stand in the way of sharing your knowledge, passion and voice with the world. Visit the link below and start reading *Introduction to Podcast Technology* today!

http://podcasttechnologybook.com

65914030R00069

Made in the USA
San Bernardino, CA
07 January 2018